CANON EOS R100
POCKET GUIDE

TABLE OF CONTENTS

01 PRE-SHOOT CHECKLIST

Check these settings before you head out with your camera!

SETTING	MY PREFERRED SETTING
☑ Shooting Mode	
☑ White Balance Setting	
☑ ISO Setting	
☑ Exposure Compensation	
☑ Focus Mode	
☑ Focus Method	
☑ Drive Mode	
☑ Metering Mode	
☑ Picture Style	
☑ Bracketing Setting	
☑ File Format: JPEG/HEIF, or RAW & JPEG/HEIF	
☑ Battery Fully Charged and In Camera	
☑ Memory Card Formatted and In Camera	

02 BUTTONS, DIALS, AND SCREENS

CAMERA BODY TOP

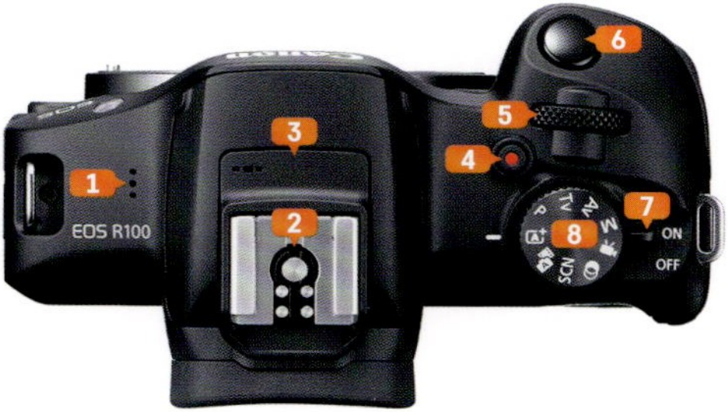

1. **Speaker:** When playing back movies, turn the Main dial to adjust the speaker volume.
2. **Multi-Function Shoe:** External flash units and other accessories can be mounted here.
3. **Built-In Flash:** Open manually by pulling up on the front of the flash.
4. **Movie Shooting Button:** Press to start recording a movie.
5. **Main Dial:** Use this dial to set the shutter speed, aperture, and other settings.

6. **Shutter Button:** Press halfway to activate autofocus, press all the way to take photo.

7. **Power Switch:** Turns the camera on and off.

8. **MODE Dial:** Turn the dial to select the Shooting mode.

CAMERA BODY BACK

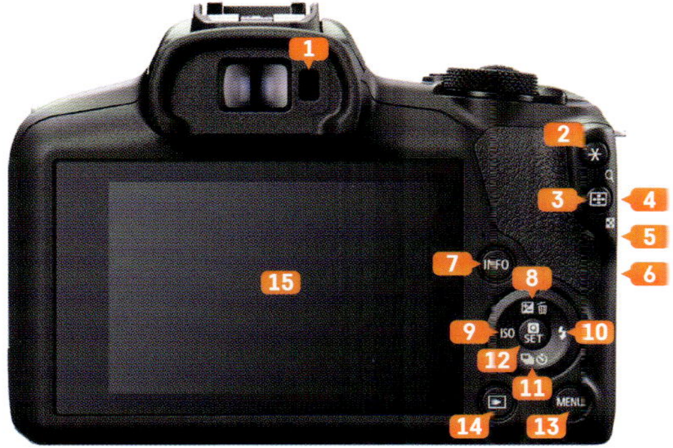

1. **Viewfinder Sensor:** Senses when you're looking through the viewfinder and activates viewfinder display.

2. **AE Lock/FE Lock/Magnify Button:** When pressed, locks the exposure/Locks the flash exposure when using the flash/Zooms into photo when reviewing photos.

3. **AF Point Selection/Index/Reduce Button:** Press to pick AF point/ Show the index of images on memory card/Zoom out on selected image.

4. **Digital Terminal (under cover on side):** USB C terminal used to connect the camera to a computer.

5. **HDMI Out (under cover on side):** HDMI micro connection used to output video.

6. **DC Cord Hole (on side):** Used to power camera.

7. **INFO Button:** Press to cycle through views displaying different information.

8. **Up/Exposure Compensation/Erase Button:** Used to navigate menus and select or change options/Used to set exposure compensation/ Erase photo or movie on screen during playback.

9. **Left/ISO Button:** Used to navigate menus and select or change options/Select ISO.

10. **Right/Flash button:** Used to navigate menus and select or change options/Set flash mode.

11. **Down/Self-Timer/Drive Mode Selection Button:** Used to navigate menus and select or change options/Set drive mode.

12. **Quick Control (Q) / Setting (SET) Button:** Use to access the Quick Control screen/Use to finalize a setting and return to a previous screen.

13. **MENU Button:** Press to bring up Menu options.

14. **Playback Button:** Press to view the last image/movie taken.

15. **Screen:** Displays multiple features, options, and settings for shooting and playback.

CAMERA BODY FRONT

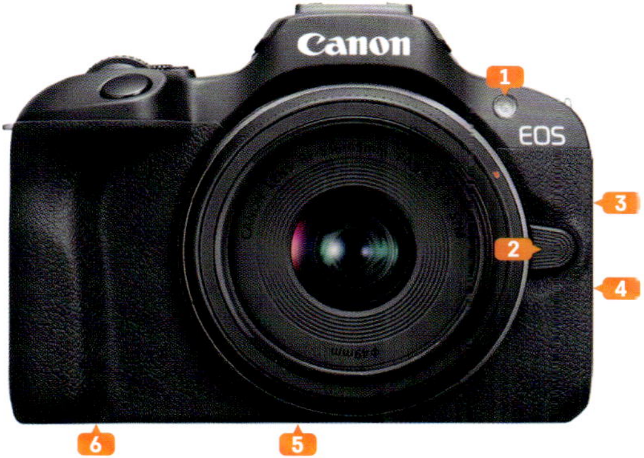

1. **AF-Assist Beam/Self-Timer/Remote Control Lamp:** Lights up area in front of camera in low light/Blinks when Self-Timer is active/Shows when remote is attached.
2. **Lens Release Button:** Press to remove lens.
3. **External Microphone Terminal (under cover on side):** Connect external microphone to camera.
4. **Remote Control Terminal (under cover on side):** Connect remote control to camera.
5. **Tripod Socket (on bottom):** Standard socket for tripod or monopod.
6. **Battery and Memory Card Compartment (on bottom):** Open to access battery and memory card compartment.

SHOOTING SCREEN (STILL PHOTO)

Each time you press the INFO button, the information display will change. The display will show only the settings currently applied.

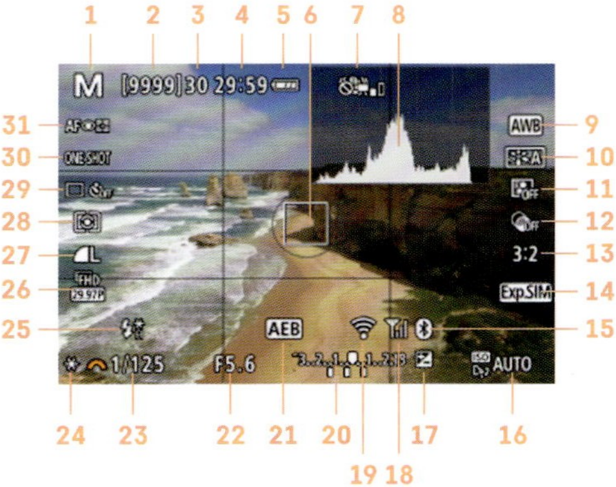

Note: Viewfinder display positions will vary for some items.

1. Shooting Mode
2. Number of Available Shots/Self Timer Countdown
3. Maximum Burst
4. Movie Recording Time Available
5. Battery Level
6. Focus Point
7. Warning to Turn Off Digital Movie IS
8. Histogram
9. White Balance
10. Picture Style
11. Auto Lighting Optimizer
12. Creative Filters
13. Still Image Aspect Ratio
14. Exposure Simulation
15. Bluetooth Function
16. ISO Speed
17. Exposure Compensation
18. Wi-Fi Signal
19. Wi-Fi Function
20. Exposure Level Indicator
21. AEB/FEB
22. Aperture Value
23. Shutter Speed
24. AE Lock
25. Flash Needed Warning (Blinking)/Flash Ready (On)/FE Lock/ High-Speed Sync
26. Movie Recording Size
27. Image Quality
28. Metering Mode
29. Drive Mode
30. AF Operation
31. AF Method

SHOOTING SCREEN (MOVIE)

Each time you press the INFO button, the information display will change. The display will show only the settings currently applied.

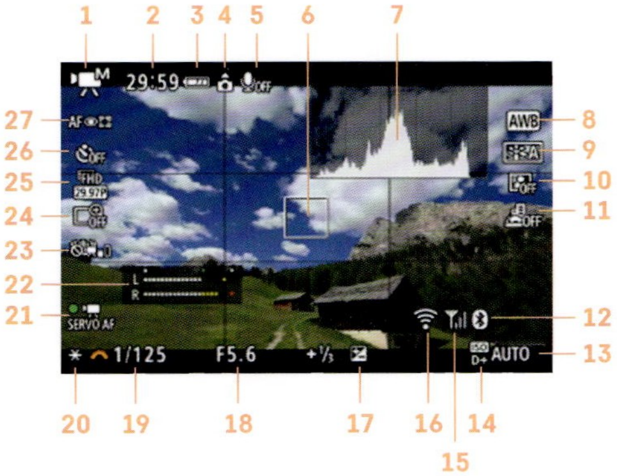

Note: Viewfinder display positions will vary for some items.

1. Shooting Mode
2. Movie Recording Time/Elapsed Recording Time
3. Battery Level
4. Shows Camera Orientation
5. Sound Recording Off Indicator
6. AF Point
7. Histogram
8. White Balance
9. Picture Style
10. Auto Lighting Optimizer
11. Miniature Effect Movie Indicator
12. Bluetooth Function
13. ISO Speed
14. Highlight Tone Priority
15. Wi-Fi Signal Strength
16. Wi-Fi Function
17. Exposure Compensation
18. Aperture Value
19. Shutter Speed
20. AE Lock
21. Movie Servo AF
22. Audio Level Recording Indicator
23. Movie Digital IS
24. Digital Zoom
25. Movie Recording Size
26. Movie Self-Timer
27. AF Method

03 ESSENTIAL MODES AND SETTINGS

SHOOTING MODES

Rotate Mode Dial to select shooting mode.

Creative Zone:

P (Program AE): The camera sets the shutter speed and aperture based on metering info and current ISO.

Tv (Time Value, or Shutter Speed Priority): You set the shutter speed and the camera sets the aperture based on metering info and current ISO.

Av (Aperture Value, or Aperture Priority): You set the aperture and the camera sets the shutter speed based on metering info and current ISO. Range of available apertures depends on the attached lens.

M (Manual): You set ISO, shutter speed, and aperture.

Basic Zone:

A+ (Scene Intelligent Auto): The camera assesses the scene and sets the optimum settings automatically. It will even adjust the focus on both still and moving subjects.

A (Hybrid Auto): You can create a short movie of your photos by shooting just still images. The camera automatically records a 2-4 second clip each time you take a photo. These are later combined into a movie clip.

SCN (Special Scene Mode): You select the proper scene from the list of 10 options and the camera adjusts the settings accordingly. You can pick from the following scene modes: Portrait, Landscape, Sports, Panning, Close-up, Food, Night Portrait, Handheld Night Scene, HDR Backlight Control, and Silent mode.

Creative Filters Mode: This mode allows you to pick one of the creative filters to be applied to your content as it's being shot. You can pick from the following: Grainy Black and White, Soft Focus, Fish-eye, Water Painting, Toy Camera, Miniature, HDR Art (Standard, Vivid, Bold, Embossed).

Movie Zone:

Movie Recording: Used to take movies.

Rotate Mode dial to Movie Recording, then Menu > Shooting [Screen 1] > Shooting Mode.

Movie Auto Exposure: Camera sets the exposure and the ISO.

Movie Manual Exposure: You pick the shutter speed, aperture, and ISO.

Note: The Shooting menu options change depending on which shooting zone is selected.

METERING MODES

Use shooting menu 2 > Metering mode

Evaluative: General-purpose mode suited for most situations and subjects (even backlit subjects).

Partial: Uses a medium area (approx. 5.8%) at the center of the screen for determining exposure. Good choice when there is very bright light around the subject.

Spot: Uses a small area (approx. 2.9%) at the center of the screen. Use when you need to meter on a specific part of the scene.

Center-Weighted Average: The camera analyzes the whole scene to determine exposure, but places more emphasis on info at the center of the screen.

EXPOSURE COMPENSATION

Press Shutter button halfway down, then press the Up Arrow/Exposure Compensation button and use the Command Dial to set the compensation from −3 (darker) to +3 (lighter) stops, in 1/3-stop increments.

Note: The exposure compensation you set will remain in effect until you change it; it does not return to 0 when the camera is turned off.

FOCUS OPERATION

MENU > Shooting (Screen 4) > Focus Mode > AF

One Shot AF: Focus starts when Shutter button is pressed halfway, then locks when focus is achieved. Best for stationary subjects.

Servo: Focus starts when Shutter button is pressed halfway and continues to focus until photo is taken. Best for moving subjects.

Note: For **Manual focus**, set the AF/MF switch on the lens to MF, and rotate the focus ring on the lens barrel to focus. For RF lenses without a focus mode switch, use Menu > Shooting (Screen 4) > Focus Mode > MF.

AUTOFOCUS METHODS

MENU > Shooting (Screen 4) > AF Method

Face + Tracking: The camera detects and focuses on faces, then tracks the face if it moves.

Spot AF: Uses the smallest possible focusing point, even smaller than 1-Point AF, for critical focus.

1-Point AF: The camera focuses using a single point.

Zone AF: Uses a wide zone AF frame to acquire focus. Gives priority to faces and items closest to the camera.

Note: Pressing the Shutter button halfway down will show you which AF points are in focus.

DRIVE MODES

MENU > Shooting (Screen 6) > Drive Mode

Single Shooting: The camera takes a single shot every time the Shutter button is pressed.

Continuous Shooting: The camera takes up to 6.5 shots a second. If the AF operation is set to Servo AF, the number of frames per second drops to 3.5.

Self-Timer 10: Sets the self-timer for 10 seconds.

Self-Timer 2: Sets the self-timer for 2 seconds.

Self-Timer Continuous Shooting: Sets the self-timer to start shooing the set number of photos starting in 10 seconds.

WHITE BALANCE

MENU > Shooting (Screen 2) > White Balance

Auto (AWB) setting is best for most situations as it uses the ambient light color to adjust the white balance for your images. **AWB-W** (Auto-White Priority) is best when you want to reduce a warm color cast. White balance can be set to shift colors warmer, cooler, or keep them accurate. Other settings are all matched to different lighting types. For truest colors, pick the type of lighting being used to illuminate scene.

FILE FORMATS

MENU > Shooting (Screen 1) > Image Quality. There are three file types used for image storage: RAW, JPEG, and HEIF.

RAW/C-RAW (Compact RAW): The RAW data from the image sensor is recorded each time a photo is taken. The C-RAW version is a compressed RAW file that takes up less space—use the Main Command Dial to set the file size.

JPEG/HEIF: Decide the size of the JPEG/HEIF (Large, Medium, Small1, or Small2) using the left and right arrow keys.

RAW/JPEG: If you have selected both a RAW and JPEG/HEIF option, the camera saves two files each time the Shutter button is pressed: a RAW file and a JPEG/HEIF file.

MOVIE RECORDING QUALITY

Set the size, frame rate, and compression: Rotate Mode dial to Movie Recording, then Menu > Shooting [Screen 1] > Movie recording Size.

4K Movie Recording: Records at 3840x2160 with an aspect ratio of 16x9. Use a memory card with a fast write speed, and if a red temperature warning icon appears during recording, stop recording. Allow the card to cool before removing it from the camera. Any frame from a 4K movie recording can be saved as a JPEG still image.

FHD: Records at 1920x1080 with an aspect ratio of 16x9.

59.94 fps, 29.97 fps, or 23.98 fps: These are used when the output is designed for NTSC television.

50 fps, 25 fps: These are used when the output is designed for PAL television.

High Frame Rate Movies: You can record HD movies at a high frame rate of 119.88 fps (NTSC) or 100.00 fps (PAL) by setting Menu > Movie rec quality > High Frame Rate to Enable. This is for recording movies that will be played back in slow motion. The maximum recording time per movie is 7 minutes 29 seconds.

Compression Method:

IPB (Standard): Compresses multiple frames at a time.

ALL-I: Uses ALL-I compression for time-lapse movies. Creates larger files that are more suitable for editing.

Note: All movies are recorded using the MP4 recording format.

Note: Check the current memory card requirements and make sure you are using a fast-enough card, especially when it comes to 4K capture.

04 OTHER HELPFUL SETTINGS

EXPOSURE SIMULATION

MENU > Shooting (Screen 6) > Exposure Simulation. This feature displays a simulation of the current exposure settings as they are applied to the scene.

Enable: Image brightness is displayed to match the settings used to take the photo.

Disable: The image is displayed at the standard brightness all the time, regardless of exposure settings or exposure compensation.

PICTURE STYLES

MENU > Shooting (Screen 3) > Picture Style

Allows you to adjust settings for JPEG images. Adjustable settings are Sharpness (Strength, Fineness, Threshold), Contrast, Saturation, Color Tone, Filter Effect (Monochrome), and Toning Effect (Monochrome). Eight preset picture controls can all be adjusted: **A (Auto)**, **S (Standard)**, **P (Portrait)**, **L (Landscape)**, **FD (Fine Detail)**, **N (Neutral)**, **F (Faithful)**,

M (Monochrome). Monochrome also has four color filters: Yellow, Orange, Red, Green. Finally, there are also three User-Defined Picture Styles, which allow you to customize any of the styles for easy access.

CUSTOM WHITE BALANCE

Setting a custom White Balance can help you get the best color when you're shooting under mixed lighting:

1. Take a photo of a white card (or white wall) under the mixed lighting at the scene.
2. Select MENU > Shooting (Screen 2) > Custom White Balance.
3. Select the white image taken in Step 1: Press OK button.
4. Select MENU > Shooting (Screen 2) > White Balance, and select the Custom White Balance icon.

COLOR SPACE

MENU > Shooting (Screen 2) > Color Space

sRGB: Smaller color space. Best when images are used directly from camera.

Adobe RGB: Larger color space. Best used when images will be edited with post-processing software.

NOISE REDUCTION

MENU > Shooting (Screen 3) > Long Exposure Noise Reduction

Reduces noise in images with shutter speeds of 1 second or longer. Doubles time needed to save image to memory card. Choices are Off, Auto, and On. Auto is usually the best choice.

MENU > Shooting (Screen 3) > High ISO Speed NR

Reduces noise in images taken at high ISO settings. Use Standard for default, Low for less noise reduction, and High for more noise reduction. There is also the option to use Multi-Shot Noise Reduction: This mode uses 4 consecutive images combined into a single JPEG with the highest level of noise reduction applied. Cannot be used when the image quality is set to RAW or RAW+JPEG.

AUTO ISO

Press the ISO button (Left Arrow Cross Key), then use the Left and Right arrow keys to select an ISO between 100–12800 in 1/3 step increments (or AUTO).

You can use MENU > Shooting (Screen 1) > ISO Speed Settings to set the maximum ISO the camera will use when set to AUTO ISO.

AUTO EXPOSURE BRACKETING

You can bracket a set of three exposures up to +/-3 stops in 1/3-stop increments:

1. Select MENU > Shooting (Screen 1) > Exposure Compensation/AEB.

2. Set the Bracketing range by turning the Main dial.

3. If desired, set the exposure compensation amount by pressing the Cross Keys.

4. Press OK.

5. Take the pictures, and three bracketed shots will be created. (If you're in Single shooting drive mode, take three pictures to create the bracketed sequence. If you're in a Continuous shooting drive mode, the three shots will be taken together when you press and hold the Shutter button.)

Note: The three photos will be in the following order: Properly exposed, underexposed, and overexposed.

Note: Bracketing will remain on until you set the Bracketing range back to 0.

WIRELESS CONNECTION

Install the Camera Connect app on your smartphone and pair it with the EOS R100.

This will allow you to view and transfer images to your smartphone, see the Live View image on your smartphone, and even shoot remotely from your smartphone.

RESET CAMERA

MENU > Set-Up (Screen 4) > Reset Camera

Pick between Basic Settings (which restores the default settings for camera shooting functions and menu settings) or Other Settings (which allows for individual selected option to be reset).

HDR HDR BACKLIGHT CONTROL MODE

Combine three images to reduce contrast and improve tonal range. A single High Dynamic Range image has more details in both the highlights and the shadows.

1. Turn the Mode dial to SCN (Special Scene Mode).
2. Press OK/Set Button.
3. Choose HDR Backlight Control using the Main dial, then press the OK/Set button again.
4. Take the picture.

Note: Hold the camera as steady as possible because the camera will automatically align the three images into a final photo. Any shake or movement can cause this to not work as expected.

TIME-LAPSE MOVIES

Create a time-lapse movie in-camera:

1. Set Mode Dial to Movie Mode.
2. MENU > Shooting (Screen 3) > Time-Lapse Movie.
3. Select Scene:

   Scene 1 is for subjects like people walking.
   Scene 2 is for slowly moving subjects like clouds
   Scene 3 is for slowly changing subjects like sunrises or sunsets.
4. Select Interval/shots: Set the interval by using the left and right arrow keys.
5. Set the Number of Shots you'd like to take for the time-lapse movie.
6. Select the movie Recording size: 4K or FHD.
7. Select Auto Exposure to choose the shooting method:

   Fixed 1st Frame: The first shot is metered, then all subsequent shots match that first shot's exposure.
   Each Frame: Each frame is metered and shot separately.
8. In the Screen Auto Off option, choose Disable to have the image displayed (though the screen will automatically turn off 30 minutes after the time-lapse shooting begins); choose Enable to have the screen turn off 10 seconds after the time-lapse shooting begins.

9. Choose whether you'd like to hear beep(s) after every image is captured (Beep per Image Taken).

10. Once all these settings are selected, press MENU to turn off the menu screen.

11. Press the Movie Shooting button, then press the Shutter button to start shooting the time-lapse movie.

Note: You can press the INFO button at any time during time-lapse shooting to turn on and off the screen.

06 TYPICAL SHOOTING SCENARIOS

SHOOTING SCENARIO
PORTRAIT

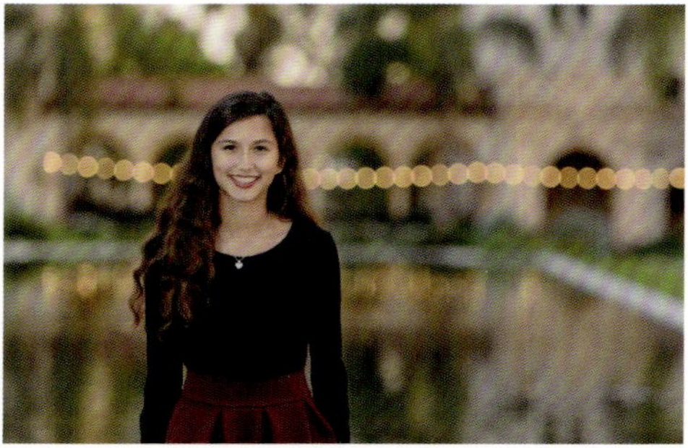

KEY PRINCIPLES

- The key to a portrait like this is shallow depth of field. So shoot in **APERTURE PRIORITY (Av)** mode and start with the lowest aperture your lens offers (such as **f/2.8 or f/4**).
- Remember to **focus on the eyes**.

- If the image is too dark or too light, use **EXPOSURE COMPENSATION** to adjust the brightness level.
- If the image is blurry from a slow shutter speed, **raise the ISO** to increase your sensor's sensitivity to light, thus allowing for a faster shutter speed.
- Remember to use a **focal length of 50mm or greater** so that you don't distort your subject's face.

SHOOTING SCENARIO
GROUP PORTRAIT

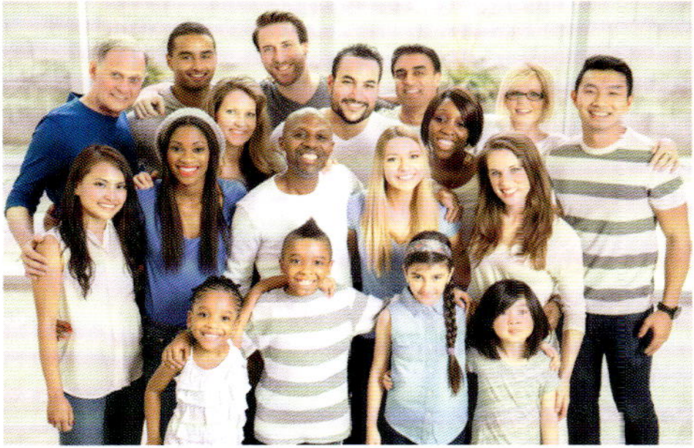

KEY PRINCIPLES

- In order to get everyone in focus, you need a deep depth of field. So shoot in **APERTURE PRIORITY (Av)** mode and set the aperture between **f/8–f/16**.
- **Focus on the person in the middle of the group**. Check the focus by using the LCD screen. View it at 100% and check faces in the front and back rows. If anyone is out of focus, use a smaller aperture for deeper depth of field.
- Use **EVALUATIVE METERING** to account for the light in the entire scene.
- **Arrange the group so they can all see you** (and you can see them).
- Use **EXPOSURE COMPENSATION** if the image is too bright or too dark.
- If image is blurry, **raise the ISO** to allow the camera to use a faster shutter speed.

SHOOTING SCENARIO

LANDSCAPE

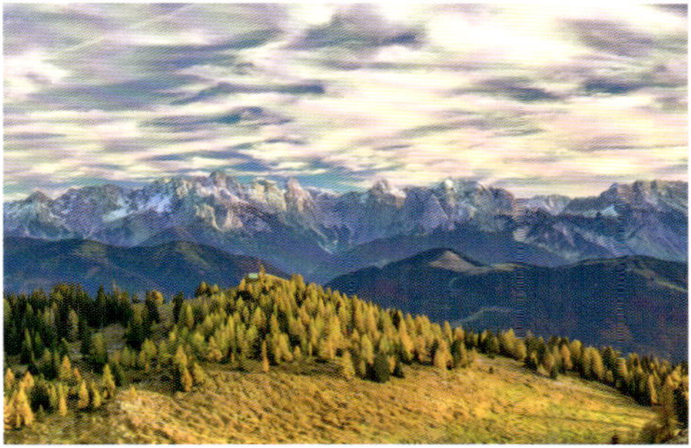

KEY PRINCIPLES

- Shoot in **APERTURE PRIORITY (Av) mode** to control depth of field, and start with **f/16** to ensure deep depth of field.
- **Use a tripod** to eliminate camera movement.
- Use **EVALUATIVE METERING** and **ONE-SHOT AF** focus mode.
- **Set the ISO to a low setting (100–200)** to avoid any digital noise.
- Shoot in **RAW** so that you have the most available information when editing later.
- Consider **AEB BRACKETING** your exposures.

SHOOTING SCENARIO

FREEZE ACTION

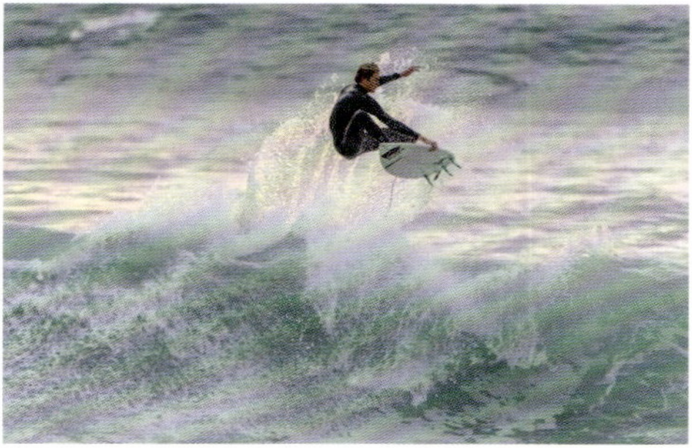

KEY PRINCIPLES

- Use **SHUTTER PRIORITY (Tv)** mode and set the shutter speed to a value that will freeze the action. The appropriate shutter speed depends on your subject and its movement, but could be anywhere between **1/500–1/4000 sec**.
- Use **Continuous Shooting**: This shoots in the highest frame rate and will help in capturing the fast action.
- Use **SERVO** autofocus so that the camera keeps focusing as the subject moves.
- If the image is dark or blurry, **raise the ISO** or try AUTO ISO to automatically have the camera adjust the ISO as needed.

SHOOTING SCENARIO

SHOWING MOTION—PANNING

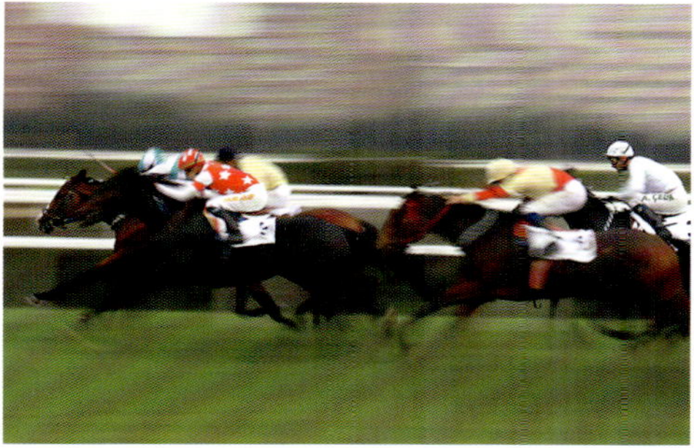

KEY PRINCIPLES

- Shoot in **SHUTTER PRIORITY (Tv)** mode and use a slow-enough shutter speed to allow for the subject to move during the exposure.
- **Follow the subject** across the frame as you shoot.
- Use **SERVO** autofocus, as well as the **Zone AF** focus method to ensure the camera focuses on the subject.

SHOOTING SCENARIO

LOW-LIGHT ACTION

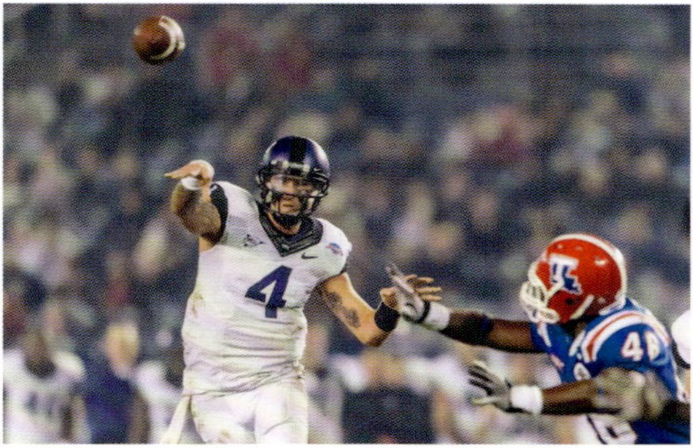

KEY PRINCIPLES

- Shoot in **APERTURE PRIORITY (Av)** mode and use a wide aperture such as **f/2.8 or f/4**.
- Use **PARTIAL METERING** and meter on the subject's face.
- Use **SERVO** autofocus and **1-POINT AF** (a single focus point).
- **Set the ISO to 1600 or higher**, depending on the amount of available light.
- If the image is blurry, **increase the ISO** to allow for a faster shutter speed.

SHOOTING SCENARIO

LONG EXPOSURE

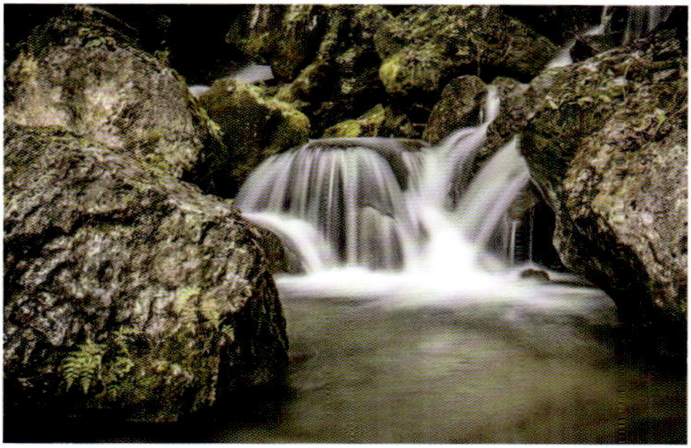

KEY PRINCIPLES

- Use **MANUAL** shooting mode, which allows you to use the **BULB** shutter speed for long exposures.
- **Use a tripod** to keep the camera stable.
- Use the **ONE-SHOT AF** focus mode, or try manual focus if the camera is having a hard time locking on focus
- **Use a low ISO** (100–400) and **shoot RAW** to ensure a high-quality file.
- Use a **remote release** with a lock to avoid touching (shaking) the camera.

SHOOTING SCENARIO
MACRO/CLOSE-UP

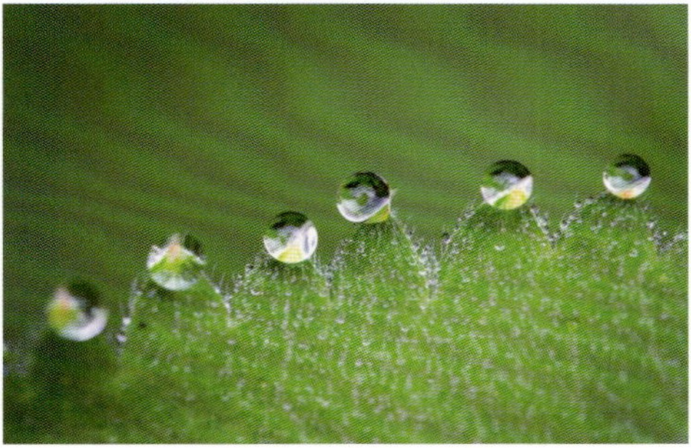

KEY PRINCIPLES

- Shoot in **APERTURE PRIORITY (Av)** mode and **use a small aperture** to ensure you achieve enough depth of field (this image was shot at f/13).
- Use **EVALUATIVE METERING** to analyze the light in the entire frame.
- A **tripod** is very useful for keeping the camera steady.
- Use **MANUAL FOCUS** and **zoom in** to confirm your focus is tack-sharp.

- Try using a dedicated **macro lens** or **close-up filters** to make sure you can achieve sharp focus when you're so close to the subject.

SHOOTING SCENARIO

VIDEO RECORDING/VLOGGING

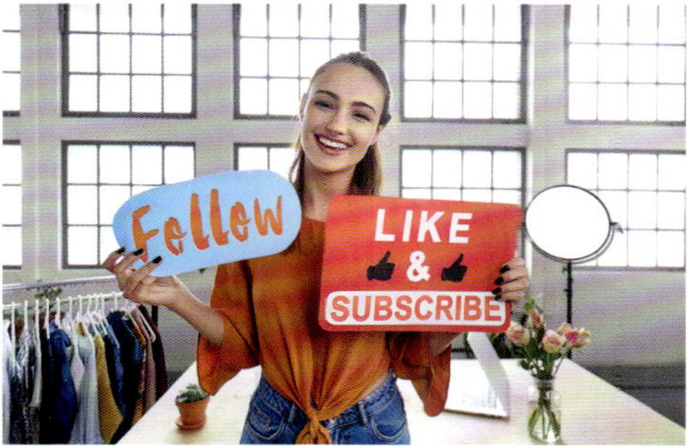

KEY PRINCIPLES

- Use a **shallow depth of field** to keep the viewers' attention on the subject. A **wide aperture** will keep the subject in focus while having the area in front of and behind the subject fall out of focus.

- Consider using **23.98 fps** for a more cinematic look. This is selected in Menu > Shooting 1 > Movie Recording Size.
- Try setting the **shutter speed** to **twice the frame rate**, or as close as you can get. If using 23.98 fps, the shutter speed should be 1/50 (or 1/60) second.
- Consider using an **external microphone** for better sound. For example, Canon makes the DM-E100 or the DM-E1, both of which are compatible with the R100.
- Keep the camera stable with a **tripod or gimble**. Smooth footage looks more professional.
- Remember to leave a second of two of empty footage at the beginning and end of your video clips, making them much easier to edit later.